weblinks

You don't need a computer to use this book. But, for readers who do have access to the Internet, the book provides links to recommended websites which offer additional information and resources on the subject.

You will find weblinks boxes like this on some pages of the book.

---
weblinks

For more information about Johnny Depp, go to www.waylinks.co.uk /21CentLives/FilmStars
---

waylinks.co.uk

To help you find the recommended websites easily and quickly, weblinks are provided on our own website, **waylinks.co.uk**. These take you straight to the relevant websites and save you typing in the Internet address yourself.

Internet safety

↗ Never give out personal details, which include: your name, address, school, telephone number, email address, password and mobile number.

↗ Do not respond to messages which make you feel uncomfortable – tell an adult.

↗ Do not arrange to meet in person someone you have met on the Internet.

↗ Never send your picture or anything else to an online friend without a parent's or teacher's permission.

↗ If you see anything that worries you, tell an adult.

A note to adults
Internet use by children should be supervised. We recommend that you install filtering software which blocks unsuitable material.

Website content

The weblinks for this book are checked and updated regularly. However, because of the nature of the Internet, the content of a website may change at any time, or a website may close down without notice. While the Publishers regret any inconvenience this may cause readers, they cannot be responsible for the content of any website other than their own.

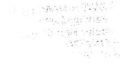

WAYLAND

21st CENTURY LIVES
FILM STARS

Liz Gogerly

TOWER HAMLETS
Learning Centre
Poplar High Street
LONDON
E14 0AF

WAYLAND

Editors: Kirsty Hamilton / Sarah Gay
Design: Peter Bailey for Proof Books
Cover design: Hodder Children's Books

Published in Great Britain in 2006 by Hodder Wayland,
an imprint of Hodder Children's Books.

Reprinted in 2006 and 2008 by Wayland, an imprint of Hachette Children's Books

The right of Liz Gogerly to be identified as the author of the work has been asserted
by her in accordance with the Copyright, Designs and Patents Act 1988.

British Library Cataloguing in Publication Data
Gogerly, Liz
Film Stars. - (21st century lives)
1.Motion picture actors and actresses - Biography -
Juvenile literature
1.Title
791.4'3'028'0922

ISBN-10: 0750248106
ISBN-13: 9780750248105

Cover: Halle Berry clutches her 'best actress' Oscar in 2002.

Picture acknowledgements: Cover Kevin Sullivan/Orange County Register/Corbis ;
4 Dan Herrick/ZUMA/Corbis; 5 Warner Bros/ZUMA/Corbis; 6 Reuters/CORBIS;
7 Miramax Films/ZUMA/Corbis; 8 Daniel A. Anderson/Orange County
Register/Corbis; 9 Doane Gregory/Warner Bros./Bureau L.A. Collections/Corbis;
10 David Bebber/Reuters/Corbis; 11 Mitchell Gerber/Corbis; Title page and 12
Stephane Cardinale/People Avenue/Corbis; 13 Corbis Sygma; 14 John
Schults/Reuters/Corbis; 15 Odeon Films/ZUMA/Corbis; 16 Frank Trapper/Corbis;
17 Corbis Sygma; 18 Rufus F. Folkks/Corbis; 19 Columbia Pictures/ZUMA/Corbis; 20
Paul Mounce/Corbis; 21 Jonathan Hession/Touchstone/Bureau L.A. Collections/Corbis

Printed in China

Hachette Children's Books
338 Euston Road
London NW1 3BH

Contents

Johnny Depp   4

Nicole Kidman   6

Halle Berry   8

Tom Cruise   10

Leonardo DiCaprio   12

Kate Winslet   14

Russell Crowe   16

Will Smith   18

Keira Knightley   20

Other Film Stars   22

Index   24

Some definitions:

BAFTAs
Awards given each year by the British Academy of Film and Television Arts for outstanding contribution to entertainment.

Golden Globes
Awards given each year by the Hollywood Foreign Press Association for the best contributions to motion pictures and television.

Oscars
Awards given each year by the Academy of Motion Picture Arts and Sciences for outstanding individual or collective efforts in film. (The awards ceremony began in 1927. Officially known as the Academy Award of Merit, nobody knows why the award was given the nickname the Oscar.)

Johnny Depp
Cool Character

Johnny loves to spend time in Britain. He particularly likes British humour and appeared in the comedy series The Fast Show.

❝I want to do kiddie movies now. I'm fed up with adult movies – most of them stink. ...But since having kids and watching lots of animated cartoons and all those great old Disney films, I think they're better, they're much better. They're more fun and they take more risks. Even things like Shrek – it's really funny and well made and intelligent. ❞

Daily Telegraph Magazine 8/3/02

Name: John Christopher Depp II

Date and place of birth: 9 June 1963, Owensboro, Kentucky, USA

Education: Dropped out of high school aged fifteen.

Big break: Johnny's first film role was in *A Nightmare On Elm Street* in 1984.

Famous films: *Edward Scissorhands* (1990), *Ed Wood* (1994), *Donnie Brasco* (1997), *Fear and Loathing in Las Vegas* (1998), *Sleepy Hollow* (1999), *Pirates of the Caribbean: The Curse of the Black Pearl* (2003), *Finding Neverland* (2004), *Charlie and the Chocolate Factory* (2005), *Pirates of the Caribbean: The Dead Man's Chest* (2006)

Acting style: Interesting and unpredictable, Johnny is drawn to unusual characters. He brings something different and exciting to each of his roles. When he played Edward Scissorhands he was inspired by the behaviour of dogs. Jack Sparrow in *Pirates of the Caribbean* was partly based on the Rolling Stones guitarist, Keith Richards. Some actors are well known for playing themselves in every film, but you never quite know who you will get with Johnny.

Top awards: Oscar nominations for *Pirates of the Caribbean* and *Finding Neverland*.

Star quality: Johnny is cool. He started life as a rock musician. He owns a nightclub and he's dated some of the most beautiful actresses and models in the world. Despite his fame and fortune Johnny still seems to be a natural, genuinely nice person.

Something you might not know about him: He is part Navajo Indian.

Johnny Depp is one of the most exciting and interesting actors in the movies. As Jack Sparrow, the roguish captain in *Pirates of the Caribbean*, he showed his comic genius. In *Finding Neverland* he sensitively portrayed J. M. Barrie, the author of *Peter Pan*. Then in 2005 he played the wonderfully eccentric Willy Wonka of Roald Dahl's *Charlie and the Chocolate Factory*.

Johnny delves deep into his imagination to bring his unusual characters to life. But as a young boy growing up in Florida, Johnny dreamed of being a rock musician. At sixteen he played guitar with a group called The Kids. The band moved to Los Angeles but never made it big. In LA, Johnny was introduced to the actor Nicolas Cage who persuaded him to try acting instead. In 1984 Johnny was snapped up at his first audition to play a part in the cult horror film, *A Nightmare on Elm Street*.

Johnny's career has never looked back. A run in the US television series *21 Jump Street* turned him into a heart-throb. He starred in a string of teen movies but claimed he felt trapped by his image as a teen idol. Then in 1990 he took the title role in the film *Edward Scissorhands*. Playing the innocent and gentle Edward showed everybody that there was more to Johnny than just a pretty face. He was offered more serious roles in classics such as *Ed Wood*, *Donnie Brasco* and *Sleepy Hollow*.

Johnny's life off-screen is almost as famous as his career on-screen. In the early years, fans loved his bad-boy image. Turning up at award ceremonies in scruffy jeans and trashing hotel rooms seemed to add to his appeal. His love affairs and engagements were always in the press. These days he lives a quieter life. When he isn't working he spends much of his time with his French actress girlfriend Vanessa Paradis and their two young children, Lily-Rose and Jack.

Johnny as Willy Wonka in Charlie and the Chocolate Factory.

"He's so talented. He may not be Tom Cruise or Tom Hanks or any other Tom …. he chooses interesting material and he doesn't want to be an icon …. Johnny surprises me; I don't know what he's going to do next, I don't know where it's going to go sometimes, and nor does he."

Film director, Terry Gilliam
Daily Telegraph Magazine 8/3/02

weblinks

For more information about Johnny Depp, go to
www.waylinks.co.uk/21CentLives/FilmStars

Nicole Kidman
The Glamorous Movie Star

As a teenager Nicole was know as Storky because she was so tall.

“ But yeah, the thing I love about *Bewitched*, why I watched it as a child, is that I always wanted to be able to do magic, so now I get to be able to do it. And you can't do Grace [*The Others*] and then Anna [*Birth*] and Virginia Woolf [*The Hours*] and all of those things without some breathers at times, because balance is important as well. **”**

The Independent 5/11/04

Name: Nicole Mary Kidman

Date and place of birth: 20 June 1967, Honolulu, Hawaii, USA

Education: Dropped out of high school to study acting at the Australian Theatre for Young People in Sydney, Australia. Later she attended St Martin's Youth Theatre in Melbourne, Australia.

Big break: In 1983 she made her film debut in *Bush Christmas*. Her first Hollywood break came in *Dead Calm* in 1989.

Famous films: *Far and Away* (1992), *Batman Forever* (1995), *To Die For* (1995), *Portrait of a Lady* (1996), *Eyes Wide Shut* (1999), *The Others* (2001), *Moulin Rouge!* (2001), *The Hours* (2002), *Cold Mountain* (2003), *The Stepford Wives* (2004), *Birth* (2004), *Bewitched* (2005), *The Interpreter* (2005)

Acting style: Sleek and intelligent, Nicole brings something different to each character she plays. She made us laugh and cry as she danced and sang her way through *Moulin Rouge!* She sent tingles of fear down our spines when she played a nervous mother living in a haunted house in *The Others*. In *The Hours* she stretched her performance to portray the depressive author Virginia Woolf.

Top awards: An Oscar for best actress for *The Hours*. She's also scooped a BAFTA and 3 Golden Globes.

Star quality: A true professional who isn't scared to take risks. To play Virginia Woolf in *The Hours* she wore an unflattering false nose. She is also left-handed but learned to write with her right hand for the part. In *Moulin Rouge!* she did the high-wire routines herself.

Something you might not know about her: In 2004 she brought movie star glamour to the advertisement for the perfume Chanel Number 5. Her short appearance turned her into the highest-paid person to star in a TV commercial ever.

Nicole plays Ada Monroe in the epic film Cold Mountain.

For and earned her first Golden Globe. At last, Nicole had shown everyone there was more to her than just being Mrs Tom Cruise.

The couple starred together for one last time in 1999, in the thriller *Eyes Wide Shut*. It came as quite a surprise when the couple split in 2001. Following this, Nicole had some fantastic roles to keep her busy. The dancing classes she had as a child stood her in good stead for her part in *Moulin Rouge!*. What followed was a spectacular performance which earned her another Golden Globe and an Oscar nomination. The same year she brought quiet intensity to her part in the ghost story *The Others*.

In 2002 Nicole finally scooped an Oscar for best actress for the film *The Hours*. Since then she has become a box office hit. In 2005 she 'bewitched' her audiences again playing Isabel, a witch who finds herself in the re-make of the classic 1960s television series *Bewitched*. Nicole married Australian country singer Keith Urban on June 25 2006 in Sydney, Australia.

Blessed with striking red hair and pale skin, Nicole was never one for basking in her native Australian sunshine. Growing up in Longueville in Sydney, she spent most of her teenage years in the theatre practising acting. She made her film debut in the Australian film *Bush Christmas* when she was just sixteen.

In 1989 Nicole caught critics' eyes in the USA when she starred in the thriller *Dead Calm*. The following year she played alongside superstar Tom Cruise in *Days of Thunder*. By the end of the year Nicole and Tom were married, becoming one of the most glamorous couples in Hollywood. In 1992 they starred together in the romantic film *Far and Away*. However, Nicole was always determined to strike out alone. In 1995 she impressed critics with her comic performance in *To Die*

"I was never convinced before I met her, before we started talking about this project. But as soon as I met her, she just knew what we were going for. She really digs down deep inside. She's impeccable."

Jonathan Glazer, director of *Birth* (2004)
The Independent 5/11/04

weblinks

For more information about Nicole Kidman, go to
www.waylinks.co.uk/21CentLives/FilmStars

Halle Berry
Hollywood's Golden Girl

Halle punches the air as she accepts the Oscar for best actress in 2002.

"Oh, my God. Oh, my God. I'm sorry. This moment is so much bigger than me. This moment is for...every nameless, faceless woman of colour that now has a chance because this door tonight has been opened. "

Taken from Halle's speech on Oscar night 2002.

Name: Halle Maria Berry

Date and place of birth: 14 August 1966, Cleveland, Ohio, USA

Education: Sailed through high school, becoming class president, editor of the school magazine and prom queen. Dropped out of college where she was studying journalism to seek a career in modelling.

Big break: Playing a drug addict in Spike Lee's *Jungle Fever* (1991).

Famous films: X-Men (2000), *Swordfish* (2001), *Monster's Ball* (2002), *Die Another Day* (2002), X-2 (2003), *Gothika* (2003), *Catwoman* (2004), *X-Men: The Last Stand* (2006)

Acting style: Stole the show with her passion and emotion in *Monster's Ball* (2002). Can also turn her hand to comedy in classics such as *The Flintstones* (1994). Good all-round action heroine too – check out her parts in *X-Men* (2000), *Swordfish* (2001), *Die Another Day* (2002), X-2 (2003) and *Catwoman* (2004).

Top awards: Oscar for best actress in 2002 for her part in the film *Monster's Ball* (2002).

Star quality: Brains and beauty. Believe it or not, she's down to earth too.

Something you might not know about her: In 1996 Halle became the new face of the cosmetic company Revlon. She turned down similar jobs advertising beauty products for black women. Halle claimed she wanted to promote products that worked for every woman. She is also a diabetic.

Halle plays the action heroine as Catwoman in 2004.

Halle was born in Cleveland, Ohio to an African American father and a white mother. Halle's father was a heavy drinker who physically abused Halle's mother and sister. He left the family home when Halle was four. Halle's mother struggled to raise her daughters but encouraged Halle to do well at school. As well as being gifted academically, Halle stood out because she was very pretty. Aged seventeen she won the first of many beauty pageants and in 1987 came third in the Miss World Contest. After school she briefly attended college but dropped out to become a model in Chicago. When modelling didn't work out, Halle moved to New York to try acting.

Halle's big break came in Spike Lee's *Jungle Fever*. For once, her lovely looks were a great obstacle. Spike thought she was too beautiful to play a drug addict. Halle didn't take 'no' for an answer. To convince Spike that she could play the part she lived on the street with real drug addicts. When the director of *The Flintstones* overlooked Halle for the part of the secretary Sharon Stone, Halle took action again. This time she told the director that the Flintstone town of Bedrock needed to be racially integrated.

In the early days Halle struggled to win parts but now she's in top demand. In 1996 she became the first black actress to earn $1 million for her part in *Executive Decision*. Today, she is one of Hollywood's highest earners, starring in blockbusting films such as the James Bond film *Die Another Day*. In 2004 she slinked onto the screen as *Catwoman*. At last, Halle was top of the bill and she didn't have to fight to get there.

"She's a combination of formidable actress with a sense of social fairness, genuine humility and she has a great sense of humor about herself."

Warren Beatty
Halle Berry: A Stormy Life by Frank Sanello
Virgin Books 2003

When Halle Berry won the Oscar for best actress in 2002 she looked every part the Hollywood star. That night she made history by becoming the first black actress to win the award.

weblinks

For more information about Halle Berry, go to
www.waylinks.co.uk/21CentLives/FilmStars

Tom Cruise
All-out Action Hero

Tom is well-known for spending time talking to his fans at film premieres.

❝I've had a very interesting life. There are ways of handling the complexities. I'm willing to take on responsibilities as a father, as a producer, as an actor - and I enjoy that. I've always been changing and evolving and growing. There's no pinnacle of power where you can sit back and rest. ❞

International Movies Database (www.imdb.com)

Name: Tom Cruise (born Thomas Cruise Mapother IV)

Date and place of birth: 3 July 1962, Syracuse, New Jersey, USA

Education: Tom's family moved frequently when he was a child. By the time he was fourteen he'd already attended fifteen different schools. One of his many schools was the St Francis Seminary in Cincinnati where he studied to become a Catholic priest.

Big break: The teen movie *Endless Love* (1981) starring Brooke Shields.

Famous films: *Risky Business* (1983), *Top Gun* (1986), *Rain Man* (1988), *Born on the Fourth of July* (1989), *Days of Thunder* (1990), *A Few Good Men* (1992), *Interview with the Vampire* (1994), *Mission: Impossible* (1996), *Jerry Maguire* (1996), Mission: Impossible II (2000), *Vanilla Sky* (2001), *Minority Report* (2002), *The Last Samurai* (2003), *Collateral* (2004), *War of the Worlds* (2005), Mission: Impossible III (2006)

Acting style: Controlled with tense outbursts. Tom is an all-out action hero. He's as at home dodging bullets and bombs as he is screeching around corners in nail-biting car chases.

Top awards: He's been nominated for an Oscar many times but Tom is yet to scoop the big one. He does have a few Golden Globes, notably for his part in *Born on the Fourth of July*.

Star quality: Effortlessly charming, Tom is renowned for his dazzling smile.

Something you might not know about him: At school Tom was very shy. He also battled with dyslexia.

Any film with Tom Cruise's name in the credits is sure to be a winner. He hit the big time in 1986 when he starred as a fighter pilot in *Top Gun*. By 1996 he'd become the first actor to star in a run of five films that grossed $100 million in the USA alone. Life began in Syracuse, New Jersey. When he was twelve his parents were divorced. Tom stayed with his mother and three sisters. Money was tight for many years and Tom had to do a paper round to help the family. He struggled through school but threw himself into sport and acting. At eighteen he left school and went to New York to pursue his dream of being an actor. The next year his break came in *Endless Love*, but it was the teen movie *Risky Business* (1983) that really launched his career.

Film critics have often accused Tom of playing the same part again and again. The 'Generic Tom Cruise Character' begins the film as cocky and self-assured (see *Top Gun*, *Jerry Maguire* and *The Last Samurai*). Somewhere in the middle of the film he has an explosive moment of self-realisation. By the end of the movie Tom's character has come full circle and developed into a more humble human being.

In his own life Tom is more complex. He is well known for his great sense of humour, his support of charities and his religious beliefs (Tom has been a member of the Church of Scientology since 1990). Yet, he has a ruthless streak too. Nobody knows why his ten-year marriage to the actress Nicole Kidman suddenly ended in divorce. When newspapers tried to speculate about his marriage and his private life he sued them. Tom is also a daredevil who loves to skydive, scuba-dive and fly. In his personal and public life Tom likes to be the winner every time. Tom had a baby girl, Suri, on April 18 2006 with American actress Katie Holmes.

On the run. Tom makes a getaway in Vanilla Sky.

"He was one of the better people I've met in the business… Smart, funny. No sense of, like, 'I am the star' to him"

Screen writer Ron Moore, who worked with Tom on *Mission: Impossible II*. FilmForce.ign.com

11

Leonardo DiCaprio
Titanic Superstar

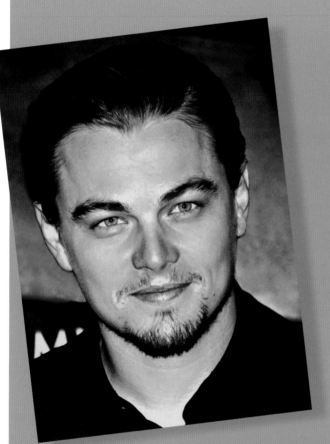

In 2003 Leo was guest editor on the Children's National Geographic Magazine.

> **"** I love the work. I love being able to get into different characters' minds and become a different person. Each movie is a unique experience and an education in a different way. It's almost like it's been my college. That's what it's been like ever since I was 16 and did *This Boy's Life*. **"**

The Independent 5/1/03

Name: Leonardo Wilhelm DiCaprio

Date and place of birth: 11 November 1974, Los Angeles, California, USA

Education: Attended the Center for Enriched Studies in LA – a school for gifted children. Later he enrolled at the John Marshall High School but earned the nickname Leonardo Retardo for doing so badly in class.

Big break: At eleven he starred as a homeless boy in the teen comedy television series *Growing Pains*. His first major film role was in *This Boy's Life* in 1993.

Famous films: *What's Eating Gilbert Grape* (1993), *Total Eclipse* (1995), *Romeo and Juliet* (1996), *Titanic* (1997), *The Beach* (2000), *Gangs of New York* (2002), *Catch Me If You Can* (2002), *The Aviator* (2004), *The Departed* (2006).

Acting style: The camera seems to love Leo but as he grows older he is proving to be a versatile and interesting actor. In *The Aviator* he ages from eighteen to forty-two years-old when he plays the eccentric millionaire businessman, film director and aviator, Howard Hughes.

Top awards: In 2005 Leo received a Golden Globe for best actor for his part in *The Aviator*, and was also nominiated for an Oscar for this role.

Star quality: A zest for life and boyish charm.

Something you might not know about him: He donated a 'huge' amount to UNICEF to help the children that had been orphaned in Thailand following the tsunami of December 2004. He is also actively involved in promoting green issues.

'I'm the king of the world!' shouted Leonardo DiCaprio in one of the most famous scenes from *Titanic*, perhaps the biggest box office hit of all time. Now that Leo has won a Golden Globe and an Oscar nomination for best actor for the part of Howard Hughes in *The Aviator*, he is recognised as Hollywood royalty.

Leo was named after the painter Leonardo da Vinci. Leo's mother claimed that she had felt her unborn baby kick her while she was looking at one of the great master's paintings. Leo's parents divorced when he was one but they remained friends and helped to bring Leo up in a liberal, hippy fashion.

Even from an early age Leo wanted to act. He was just sixteen when he starred alongside Robert De Niro in *This Boy's Life*. In 1993 he made his name when he played Arnie Grape, the mentally autistic brother of Johnny Depp in the low-budget movie, *What's Eating Gilbert Grape*. People were so convinced by his performance that they actually believed he was autistic. He also earned a well-deserved Oscar nomination for this role. Soon he was being offered big parts like Robin in *Batman Forever*, but Leo turned them down.

International fame came with the part of Jack in *Titanic*. Girls everywhere drooled over the latest Hollywood heart-throb. Meanwhile, male fans tried to copy the famous DiCaprio haircut. Instead of letting fame go to his head, Leo took time out from the movies. For a while, he was rarely out of the gossip columns. They made much of his love life and played up his bad boy image.

Leo's next major film was *The Beach* in 2000, but it wasn't a big success. Leo's early promise as an actor looked all but washed-up but in 2002 he starred in *Gangs of New York* and *Catch Me If You Can*. Leo was back on form. Then in 2004 he played Howard Hughes in *The Aviator*.

Leonardo in the film adaptation of best-selling novel The Beach.

"I think what Frank [the character in *Catch Me If You Can*] did in real life and what Leo does in portraying him are the same thing. They both use social camouflage. Basically, that's changing and switching occupations. I think Frank, like Leo, has a dazzling IQ. You understand in just meeting Frank how he could just pull the wool over your eyes, and there's something of that in Leo."

The film director Steven Spielberg talking about Leo's role in *Catch Me If You Can*
BBC Films

weblinks

For more information about Leonardo DiCaprio, go to
www.waylinks.co.uk/21CentLives/FilmStars

Kate Winslet
The English Rose of Cinema

Kate is often described as down-to-earth but she always looks the star at big movie events.

When asked if she had always wanted to be an actress Kate replied: **"Always. It was a matter of fact: that's what I will do. I imagined that I'd be very much a jobbing actor, a strolling player....No one was more shocked than me when I was suddenly in a movie when I was 17. And the level of excitement that I feel when I get a job that I really want is still present in me today. When Alan [Alan Parker – the director of *The Life of David Gale*] called me, there were tears and joy and dancing and immediately calling my mum! I'm still like that."**

The Independent 9/3/03

Name: Kate Elizabeth Winslet

Date and place of birth: 5 October 1975, Reading, England

Education: When she was eleven Kate enrolled at Redroofs Theatre School in Maidenhead. She left school at sixteen with 8 GCSEs.

Big break: A leading role in *Heavenly Creatures* (1994).

Famous films: *Sense and Sensibility* (1995), *Hamlet* (1996), *Titanic* (1997), *Holy Smoke* (1999), *Enigma* (2001), *Iris* (2001), The Life of David Gale (2003), *Finding Neverland* (2004), *Eternal Sunshine of The Spotless Mind* (2004), *Romance and Cigarettes* (2005), *All The King's Men* (2005)

Acting style: Warm, expressive. Kate likes a challenge and has played roles that have stretched her considerable acting ability. She will always be remembered for her romantic lead in *Titanic* but she can play funny too – see *Eternal Sunshine of the Spotless Mind*. She can also move her audience to tears – see *Jude* and *Finding Neverland*.

Top awards: In 1998 she became the youngest actress to be nominated twice for an Oscar (for *Sense and Sensibility* and *Titanic*). She was nominated again in 2002 for her part in *Iris* and twice in 2004, for best actress in *Eternal Sunshine of the Spotless Mind* and best supporting actress in *Finding Neverland*.

Star quality: Kate doesn't act the star. When she's in London she likes to take the tube. And, she's much happier in jeans and a jumper than a beautiful designer frock!

Something you might not know about her: At school Kate was teased for being overweight. Some of her classmates called her Blubber. These days Kate is proud of her curves and criticises the pressure put upon young women to be thin.

Kate Winslet shot to international fame with her leading role in the epic film *Titanic*. The feisty spirited character of Rose earned Kate an Oscar nomination for best actress. In 2005 Kate was back at the Oscars hoping to scoop an award. Many people reckon it's just a matter of time before Kate finally wins the 'big one'.

With her perfect complexion and her full lips, Kate is often called an English Rose. When she was a girl this particular English flower was teased for her fuller figure. Growing up in a bohemian family in Reading, England, Kate didn't let her figure stop her pursuing the career of her dreams. From the age of three Kate knew she wanted to be an actress and she plagued her parents to let her go to acting school. At eleven, Kate made her TV debut – in a commercial for Sugar Puffs! By thirteen she was taking small parts in TV series like *Casualty*.

Kate was just seventeen when she won her role in *Heavenly Creatures*. At the time she was working at a delicatessen. She was buttering a ham sandwich when she heard she'd got the part. Kate immediately burst into tears and had to go home. It was a great break and Kate would be highly praised for her portrayal of the near hysterical Juliet.

Next came her Oscar nominated part in Jane Austen's *Sense and Sensibility*. Kate played the flighty romantic Marianne Dashwood. The following year she made a heartbreaking Ophelia in Shakespeare's *Hamlet*. With her part of Rose in *Titanic* she showed that not only is she a fine actress but she has what it takes to be a leading movie star.

Kate is famous for being down to earth. Straight after *Titanic* she took a small part in a British film called *Plunge*. She refused a fee and even made the tea. These days she's as at home making food for her two young children as she is walking the red carpet at a film awards ceremony.

Kate with co-star Jim Carey in *Eternal Sunshine of the Spotless Mind*.

"She's amazing. We hadn't worked together before. She is so cool. There's no pretence, no weirdness, no diva… She is a great girl first, a great mum, which is impressive and made me love her even more, and obviously she is a great actress. It's so great not to have to lie about someone. I can gush on and on about Kate"

Johnny Depp, Kate's co-star in *Finding Neverland*
Q Magazine

weblinks

For more information about
Kate Winslet, go to
www.waylinks.co.uk/21CentLives/FilmStars

Russell Crowe
Rough and Ready Movie Star

Russell is well known for speaking his mind and getting into fights, but he knows when to smile for the camera.

66 **If you grow up in the suburbs of anywhere, a dream like this seems kind of vaguely ludicrous and completely unattainable. But this moment is directly connected to those imaginings. And for anybody who's on the downside of advantage, and relying purely on courage, it's possible.** 99

Crowe's acceptance speech for the Oscar for best actor for *Gladiator*.

Name: Russell Ira Crowe

Date and place of birth: 7 April 1964, Wellington, New Zealand

Education: Attended schools in Australia, returning to New Zealand aged fourteen. Dropped out of high school to form a band.

Big break: *Romper Stomper* (1992) – this Australian film brought him fame throughout Australia and New Zealand.

Famous films: *The Quick and The Dead* (1994), *Virtuosity* (1995), *LA Confidential* (1997), *Mystery, Alaska* (1999), *The Insider* (1999), *Gladiator* (2000), *Proof of Life* (2001), *A Beautiful Mind* (2002), *Master and Commander: The Far Side of the World* (2003), *Cinderella Man* (2005)

Acting style: Tough guy meets Shakespearean actor. He's quiet and moody yet his performances fill the screen. Russell also has an air of confidence that means he is a natural for playing kings and heroes.

Top awards: In 2001 he won an Oscar for best actor, for *Gladiator*. The following year he scooped a BAFTA and a Golden Globe for *A Beautiful Mind*.

Star quality: Rugged good looks. Though he appears every bit the Hollywood superstar he shuns the limelight. He prefers to spend his time living on his 560-acre farm, seven and half hours away from Sydney, Australia. Perhaps this adds to his air of mystery!

Something you might not know about him: Until recently he spent his spare time playing with his band 30 Odd Foot of Grunts. However, the band split up in May 2005 and Russell has decided to go solo.

Russell won an Oscar for his portrayal of Maximus in Gladiator.

Many movie-goers hadn't heard about Russell Crowe until he played Maximus, the mighty Roman general in the Oscar-winning movie *Gladiator*. It was a role that turned him into a superstar. Since then, Maximus has been voted the greatest movie hero of all time. Now that Pierce Brosman prepares to step down from the role as James Bond, some people think that Russell Crowe is the only actor who could go on to play the famous British spy.

The son of set caterers, Russell Crowe spent much of his childhood on film sets in Australia. By the age of six he was on the other side of the camera, playing an orphan in the Australian television series *Spyforce*. Parts in *The Young Doctors* and *Neighbours* were to follow, but when he was fourteen the family returned to New Zealand.

Meanwhile, Russell also pursued his other great love – music. At sixteen he formed a band but had to take on low-paid waiting jobs to support himself. Next came work in musicals such as *Grease* and the *Rocky Horror Show*. Russell was having fun but he wanted to explore more serious acting. After a string of Australian movies he finally got the recognition he craved in *Romper Stomper*. Russell's performance attracted the attention of American actress Sharon Stone. She bagged Russell to play the gunslinger cowboy in her next movie, *The Quick and The Dead*. At last Russell had landed on American shores. The 1995 movie, *Virtuosity*, in which he starred alongside Denzel Washington, sealed his reputation as a tough

guy. Then the part of Bud White, the seedy cop in *LA Confidential*, brought him critical acclaim. What followed, the Oscar for *Gladiator* and the Oscar nomination for *A Beautiful Mind*, brought him stardom.

Russell has become nearly as famous for his antics off-set as his wonderful performances on screen. He's outspoken and gets into fights with the press. At the same time he's very private. After the success of *Gladiator* he took off with a group of old friends on a motorcycle journey around Australia. He's the kind of person, and the type of actor, who refuses to be pinned down by anybody.

"The man exudes the physicality of a wild animal...he holds the screen with such assuredness and force, you simply can't rip your eyes away from him."

Crowe makes the cover of *Empire* magazine, May 2000 (www.nzedge.com)

weblinks

For more information about Russell Crowe, go to
www.waylinks.co.uk/21CentLives/FilmStars

Will Smith
Box Office Idol

As well as being a Hollywood star, Will is a pop icon.

Name: Willard Christopher Smith Jr.

Date and place of birth: 25 September 1968, Philadelphia, Pennsylvania, USA

Education: Overbrook High School in Pennsylvania. Turned down a scholarship to Massachusetts Institute of Technology, Boston to become a rapper.

Big break: In 1990 Will took the lead in the hugely popular television comedy *The Fresh Prince of Bel-Air*.

Famous films: *Where the Day Takes You* (1992), *Made in America* (1993), *Six Degrees of Separation* (1993), *Bad Boys* (1995), *Independence Day* (1996), *Men in Black* (1997), *Enemy of the State* (1998), *Ali* (2001), *Men in Black II* (2002), *Bad Boys II* (2003), *I, Robot* (2004), *Shark Tale* (2004), *Hitch* (2005)

Acting style: Charming action hero who can turn on the drama when he needs to. When he played the legendary heavyweight boxer Muhammad Ali his voice was so convincing that even Ali's wife Lonnie couldn't tell the difference between Will and her husband.

Top awards: Will was nominated for a Golden Globe twice for his part in *The Fresh Prince of Bel-Air*. He was also nominated for a Golden Globe and an Oscar for *Ali*. Don't forget the two Grammys he's picked up for his music either!

Star quality: This rapper turned actor has a refreshing old-fashioned approach to life. He's polite and he's a committed family man.

Something you might not know about him: He might have been the voice of Oscar in *Shark Tale* but in real life Will can't swim.

When asked about the importance of winning an Oscar, Will said:

" If I had to decide between making a movie that's going to be the biggest box office movie of the year, or winning an Oscar, I would choose box office every time. You can't fake box office. To me that's the greatest accolade you can receive – that kids all around the world are going to see your movie two, maybe three times. Never in a million years would I give up the international success of *Independence Day* or *Men in Black* for an Oscar. "

The Independent 6/10/03

Will Smith, aka 'The Fresh Prince' has that rare talent that makes the leap from being a popstar to a filmstar look so easy. Among his many achievements, he is the first hip-hop artist to be nominated for an Oscar.

In the television comedy *The Fresh Prince of Bel-Air* Will played a street-wise kid thrust into the glitzy world of Beverly Hills. Will played the part so well it was easy to believe that this was his life for real. In fact, Will was raised in West Philadelphia in a middle-class, church-going family. He even did well at school, where he picked up the nickname 'Prince' for his easy charm and ability to get himself out of trouble.

Will began rapping when he was twelve and at sixteen formed the music partnership with DJ Jazzy Jeff that would bring him international fame. Their first album *Rock the House* was an enormous hit and by the time Will was eighteen he was already a millionaire.

After the success of *The Fresh Prince of Bel-Air* came an offer of film work in *Where the Day Takes You*. Next came *Six Degrees of Separation* in which Will played a gay con man. Will showed everybody that there was more to the Prince than rapping and wise-cracks.

Will went on to star in major box office hits, including *Men in Black* and *Independence Day* (he turned down the lead in *The Matrix*). One of Will's crowning moments was playing the boxer Muhammad Ali. Will turned the part down eight times because he didn't think he was suitable. When he finally accepted the role he spent an entire year eating the same food, running the same routes and training the same way as Ali had done.
.
Will Smith is known for his positive outlook on life. He dreams hard but he's a real go-getter. In 2004 he joined Nelson Mandela in a global campaign in the fight against AIDs. He also talked about running for the presidency of the USA. The leap from rapper to president is surely the stuff of which dreams are made but with Will anything seems possible.

Will starred with Tommy Lee Jones in the hit movie Men in Black.

Muhammad Ali is asked what he thought of Will Smith in *Ali*:

Ali: I think he's a great actor. And for this role, he's the best one to do it because he looks like me a little bit and acts like me, sounds like me.

Out of his look and your look, which one of you is better-looking?

Ali: Some will say him; some people say me.

What do you say?

Ali: I say me!

The Reader's Digest, October 2002.

weblinks

For more information about
Will Smith, go to
www.waylinks.co.uk/21CentLives/FilmStars

Keira Knightley
Bright Young Thing

Keira has been described as a beautiful tomboy by movie crtics.

" **I don't think I can call myself an actress yet. I just don't think my skill level is that high. I hope that with every job it gets better. But until I'm good, I can say I'm trying to be an actor, I don't think that I've completely made it.** "

International Movies Database (www.imdb.com)

Name: Kiera Christina Knightley (she began to spell her name *Keira* when her career took off in America)

Date and place of birth: 22 March 1985, London, England

Education: Left school at sixteen with six grade As in her GCSEs. Began studying for her A levels at Esher College but left after a year because of her acting commitments.

Big break: Playing Sabé, the Decoy Queen to Queen Amidala, in *Star Wars: Episode I – The Phantom Menace* (1999).

Famous films: *Star Wars: Episode I* (1999), *Oliver Twist* (1999), *The Hole* (2001), *Princess of Thieves* (2001), *Thunderpants* (2002), *Bend It Like Beckham* (2002), *Pirates of the Caribbean: The Curse of the Black Pearl* (2003), *Love Actually* (2003), *King Arthur* (2004), *Pride and Prejudice* (2005), *The Jacket* (2005), *Pirates of the Caribbean: Dead Man's Chest* (2006), *Domino* (2006)

Acting style: Fresh, passionate and exciting. Still young, Keira is learning from each new part she plays. She shot to fame as a football crazy tomboy in *Bend It Like Beckham*. Then she turned on the charm as the damsel with attitude in the *Pirates of the Caribbean*. She even melted hearts in the romantic comedy *Love Actually*.

Top awards: An Academy Award nomination for 'Best Actress' in 2005, for her role as Elizabeth Bennett in *Pride and Prejudice*.

Star quality: Keira has movie star looks but she's very down to earth. She loves acting with a passion but is first to admit that it could all end tomorrow. If it does, Keira has talked about becoming a bricklayer.

Something you might not know about her: At school Keira was teased for being stupid. In fact she was dyslexic. Sometimes she would memorise books so that nobody would realise that she had a problem with reading.

You might say that acting is in Keira Knightley's blood. Born to actor parents, Keira was three years old when she claimed she wanted her own agent. Her parents managed to put her off for a few years but Keira was just nine years old when she made her television debut in a drama called *A Village Affair*.

Keira's parents were keen for her to continue with her education so they struck a deal that she could act during the summer holidays. Keira went on to play in quality television dramas such as E. Nesbit's *Treasure Seekers* and *Coming Home*. When filming was over it was back to school in Teddington, London, but in her spare time Keira polished her acting skills at the Heatham House Youth Club.

The part in the Star Wars movie came out of the blue but a few years later the offers of work were pouring in. In 2001 she took her first starring role in the Disney film *Princess of Thieves*. Next came a horror film called *The Hole*. Then came *Bend It Like Beckham* where she delivered an excellent performance both on and off the football pitch. Keira had expected a stunt person to play the close-ups on the pitch. When she discovered that it would have to be all her own work she launched herself into football training like a real professional. One day she practised her headers for so long that she got black eyes.

Now Keira is no stranger to action films. In *Pirates of the Caribbean* she dodged cannon balls and walked the plank. Playing Guinevere in *King Arthur* she endured axe and knife fights. Fortunately, it isn't all battlefields and sailing ships for Keira. In 2005 she gave us her very own interpretation of Elizabeth Bennett, one of Jane Austen's most popular heroines, in the film *Pride and Prejudice*. She also starred in the modern thriller, *The Jacket*.

Knight fever. Keira plays Guinevere in King Arthur.

"It's freakish how grounded she is…. If I'd trained her from the age of ten or eleven, without a shadow of doubt Keira could have been a pro. I taught her moves I've worked on with Michael Owen and he found some of them harder to master than she did."

The former Manchester United coach Simon Clifford who taught Keira to play football for her part in *Bend It Like Beckham*.
Hello! magazine.

weblinks ➤

For more information about Keira Knightley, go to
www.waylinks.co.uk/21CentLives/FilmStars

Other Film Stars

Brad Pitt

William Bradley Pitt was born on 18 December 1963 in Shawnee, Oklahoma, USA. At school he excelled in everything from sport to singing in musicals and taking part in debates. After school he attended the University of Michigan where he majored in journalism. Dreams of acting didn't kick in until he had nearly finished his degree. He left college without graduating and moved to LA to look for work as an actor.

Brad's first break was the 1991 hit *Thelma and Louise*. Starring roles in *True Romance* (1993), *Legends of the Fall* (1994), *Interview with the Vampire* (1994), *Seven* (1996), *Fight Club* (1999), *Ocean's Eleven* (2002), *Ocean's Twelve* (2004) and *Troy* (2004) have established him as one of Hollywood's biggest stars. His blonde, good looks and well-honed muscles have earned him the reputation of being a screen idol. This has sometimes clouded the fact that he is a serious actor who won a Golden Globe and was nominated for an Oscar for his powerful performance in the 1995 film *12 Monkeys*.

Orlando Bloom

Orlando Bloom shot to fame playing the character of Legolas in *The Lord of the Rings (LOTR): The Fellowship of the Ring* (2001). Since then he's appeared in the next two installments of the *LOTR* epic – *The Two Towers* (2002) and *The Return of the King* (2003). He also plays the dashing Will Turner in the *Pirates of the Caribbean* trilogy. In 2004 he starred in *Troy* and *Haven* and in 2005 he was a hit in *Elizabethtown* and *Kingdom of Heaven*.

Orlando Jonathan Blanchard Bloom was born in Canterbury, Kent, England on 13 January 1977. At school he overcame his dyslexia to pass three A levels. Orlando had ambitions of becoming an actor from an early age. The bug bit him when he realised being an actor meant playing parts like Superman or other heroes. In 1993 he moved to London to pursue his dream. In 1998 he attended the Guildhall School of Music and Drama. It was during a stage performance there that he was spotted by Peter Jackson, director of the *LOTR* trilogy.

Jude Law

Jude Law became big news in Hollywood after his starring role in the 1999 film *The Talented Mr. Ripley*. Playing the charismatic and handsome young playboy Dickie earned him an Oscar nomination for Best Supporting Actor.

David Jude Law was born on 29 December 1972 and grew up in London, England. His acting career began at the age of twelve when he joined the National Youth Music Theatre. He began television work and stage work in his teens but his break in films came in *I Love You, I Love You Not* (1996), followed by a memorable performance in *Wilde* (1997), the film about the writer Oscar Wilde.

After *The Talented Mr. Ripley* the offers of work in big budget films rolled in: *Enemy at the Gates* (2001), *AI* (2001), *Road to Perdition* (2002), *Cold Mountain* (2003). 2004 was a bumper year for Jude with starring roles in *Sky Captain and World of Tomorrow*, *Alfie* and *Lemony Snicket's A Series of Unfortunate Events*. In 2005 he was back with *All the King's Men* and *Dexterity*.

Renée Zellweger

In recent years Renée has been Oscar nominated for *Bridget Jones's Diary* (2001) and *Chicago* (2002). Then, in 2004 Renée Zellweger scooped an Oscar for best supporting actress for her part in *Cold Mountain*. Renée had finally made her mark.

Renée Kathleen Zellweger was born on 25 April 1969 in Katy, Texas, USA. She did well at school and graduated from the University of Texas with a degree in English. It was while she was at college that she discovered her talent for acting. After playing small parts in films like *Reality Bites* (1994) and *Love and a .45* (1994), Renée had her big break playing opposite Tom Cruise in *Jerry Maguire* (1996). Next came a string of lesser-known movies but in 2000 Renée starred in the hit comedies *Me, Myself & Irene* and *Nurse Betty*. Renée won a Golden Globe for her comic performance in *Nurse Betty*. In 2004 Renée was back playing Bridget in *Bridget Jones: The Edge of Reason*. Then in 2005 she starred with Russell Crowe in *The Cinderella Man*.

Cameron Diaz

Cameron Diaz hit the big screen at the age of 21 in *The Mask* (1994). She'd auditioned for the part having absolutely no previous acting experience. It was a dream start for an acting career but it was her starring role in *There's Something About Mary* (1998) that turned her into a box office sensation.

Cameron Diaz was born on 30 August 1972 in San Diego, California, USA. She spent her teenage years partying hard and travelling around the world. She was working as a model when she auditioned for *The Mask*. Next came appearances in low budget films such as *Feeling Minnesota* (1996) and *Head Above Water*

(1996). In 1997 she co-starred in *My Best Friend's Wedding*, alongside Julia Roberts. Since then her career has not looked back with starring roles in *Being John Malkovich* (1999), *Charlie's Angels* (2000), *Shrek* (2001), *Vanilla Sky* (2001), *Minority Report* (2002), *Gangs of New York* (2002), *The Sweetest Thing* (2002), *Charlie's Angels: Full Throttle* (2003), *Shrek 2* (2004) and *In Her Shoes* (2005).

Angelina Jolie

Angelina Jolie is famed for bringing computer animation Lara Croft to life. The starring role in *Lara Croft: Tomb Raider* (2001) and *Lara Croft Tomb Raider: The Cradle of Life* (2003) was all the more incredible because Angelina did all the stunts herself.

Angelina Jolie Voight was born on 4 June 1975 in Los Angeles, California, USA. Her parents are Oscar winning actor Jon Voight and actress Marcheline Bertrand. Angelina started acting aged eleven when she joined the Strasberg Theater Institute. By sixteen she was working as a model. Her early film roles were in *Cyborg 2* (1993) and *Hackers* (1995). She's gone on to win Golden Globes for her parts in the television movie *George Wallace* and *Gia*. In 1999 she won the Oscar for Best Supporting Actress for her moving performance in *Girl, Interrupted*. In 2004 she hit the big screen in *Taking Lives*, *Sky Captain and the World of Tomorrow*, *Alexander* and *Shark Tale*. As well as her colourful personal life, Angelina is famous for being a Goodwill Ambassador for the United Nations High Commission for Refugees.

Index

Academy Awards (see Oscars)
acting school 6, 14, 15, 22, 23
Ali, Muhammad 18, 19

BAFTA awards 3, 6, 16
Beatty, Warren 9
Berry, Halle 8-9
Bertrand, Marcheline 23
Bloom, Orlando 22
Brosnan, Pierce 17

Cage, Nicholas 5
Carey, Jim 15
Crowe, Russell 16-17, 23
Cruise, Tom 5, 7, 10-11, 23

De Nero, Robert 13
Depp, Johnny 4-5, 13, 15
Diaz, Cameron 23
DiCaprio, Leonardo 12-13
dyslexia 10, 20, 22

Film Stars,
    American 4-5, 8-9, 10-13, 18, 22, 23
    Australian 6-7
    British 14-15, 20-21, 22
    New Zealand 16-17

Glazer, Jonathan 7
Golden Globes 3, 6, 7, 10, 12, 13, 16, 18, 22, 23
Grammy Awards 18

Hanks, Tom 5
Hughes, Howard 12, 13

Jackson, Peter 22
James Bond 8, 9, 17
Jolie, Angelina 23

Kidman, Nicole 6-7, 11
Knightley, Keira 20-21

Law, Jude 22-23
Lee, Spike 9

modelling 8, 9, 23
Moore, Ron 11
music 4, 5, 6, 7, 16, 17, 18, 19

Oscars 3, 17, 18
    best actor 16, 17
    best actress 6, 7, 8, 9, 20
    best supporting actress 23
    nominations 4, 7, 10, 12, 13, 14, 15, 18, 19,
        20, 22, 23

Paradis, Vanessa 5
Parker, Alan 14
Pitt, Brad 22

Roberts, Julia 23

Sheilds, Brooke 10
Smith, Will 18-19
Spielberg, Steven 13
Stone, Sharon 17

television,
    commercials 6, 8, 15
    movies 23
    series 5, 12, 15, 17, 19, 20, 21
theatre 22
    musical 17, 22
    school (see acting school)

Voight, John 23

Washington, Denzel 17
Winslet, Kate 14-15

Zellweger, Renée 23